Further Problems with Pleasure

AKRON SERIES IN POETRY

AKRON SERIES IN POETRY
Mary Biddinger, Editor

Sandra Simonds, *Further Problems with Pleasure*
Leslie Harrison, *The Book of Endings*
Emilia Phillips, *Groundspeed*
Philip Metres, *Pictures at an Exhibition: A Petersburg Album*
Jennifer Moore, *The Veronica Maneuver*
Brittany Cavallaro, *Girl-King*
Oliver de la Paz, *Post Subject: A Fable*
John Repp, *Fat Jersey Blues*
Emilia Phillips, *Signaletics*
Seth Abramson, *Thievery*
Steve Kistulentz, *Little Black Daydream*
Jason Bredle, *Carnival*
Emily Rosko, *Prop Rockery*
Alison Pelegrin, *Hurricane Party*
Matthew Guenette, *American Busboy*
Joshua Harmon, *Le Spleen de Poughkeepsie*
David Dodd Lee, *Orphan, Indiana*
Sarah Perrier, *Nothing Fatal*
Oliver de la Paz, *Requiem for the Orchard*
Rachel Dilworth, *The Wild Rose Asylum*
John Minczeski, *A Letter to Serafin*
John Gallaher, *Map of the Folded World*
Heather Derr-Smith, *The Bride Minaret*
William Greenway, *Everywhere at Once*
Brian Brodeur, *Other Latitudes*

Titles published since 2008.
For a complete listing of titles published in the series,
go to www.uakron.edu/uapress/poetry.

Further Problems with Pleasure SANDRA SIMONDS

The University of Akron Press
Akron, Ohio

21 20 19 18 17   5 4 3 2 1

ISBN: 978-1-629220-59-8 (paper)
ISBN: 978-1-629220-57-4 (cloth)
ISBN: 978-1-629220-60-4 (ePDF)
ISBN: 978-1-629220-61-1 (ePub)

LIBRARY OF CONGRESS CATALOGING-IN-PUBLICATION DATA
Names: Simonds, Sandra, author.
Title: Further problems with pleasure / Sandra Simonds.
Description: Akron, Ohio : University of Akron Press, [2017] | Series: Akron series in poetry
Identifiers: LCCN 2016042859 | ISBN 9781629220598 (pbk. : alk. paper) |
  ISBN 9781629220574 (hardcover : alk. paper)
Classification: LCC PS3619.I5627 A6 2017 | DDC 811/.6—dc23
LC record available at https://lccn.loc.gov/2016042859

∞The paper used in this publication meets the minimum requirements of ANSI/NISO z39.48–1992
(Permanence of Paper).

Cover: W. Keith McManus. Reproduced with permission. Cover design by Shanna Compton.

Further Problems with Pleasure was designed and typeset in Joanna with Raleway display by Amy Freels
and printed on sixty-pound natural and bound by Bookmasters of Ashland, Ohio.

Contents

Poetry Is Stupid and I Want to Die

The one trick I've always fallen back on is to make a man think
       he's the one rejecting me
But it was so quiet in your room
       even if you had long books written by evil men
at your bedside and in your possession that deep desire
       to hurt and thus in my head scrambling between kissing you
and trying to maneuver how I would leave unharmed
       the way a woman has to manipulate both mind and body
I dreamed I was in a car and a man hit me over the head
       Please don't tell me the story of the graduate student
who put a mouse in her freezer just to "see what would happen"
       It was quiet though if even for a moment I drive around Tallahassee
to find one quiet place The way I love you is not as a sheriff
       searches for a walnut It's more violent and I can't stay in the moment
of this poem long enough for the feeling to unfold I owe the therapist
       $80 The woman wearing a fur coat with her six kids on a leash
who showed up to the South Georgia poetry reading in her stretchy jeans
       I was proud to have been the host to that
the way one might write a hallelujah ode to a black hole
       with roses and tulips shooting out of it Oh the grotesquerie

John Keats, you don't have to say "mother" anymore
       This is my quietness I am the bride and also the urn
and you are my foster child as I make you sit here
       and listen to my prayers are sweeter than any rhyme
sprouting out of a dog's skull Beautiful bud on the cold stone
       When Walter Benjamin is all high on hashish, that's when
he finally understands Poe or the lazy grass that grows along
       this lake that fakes every orgasm
and takes delight through deception
       Take these "irretrievable zones" of stupidity

which are the little wings that grow at the end of my smile
            which is I don't know Zumba? Power yoga?
Smoothies? Breakdancing? The Anthropocene is a disease
            that affects the heart lung machine is tripping
on the setting day dazed like the end of disco
            I know how to waste the mellow hour glides like a swan

into the future (so long, future!) turns into swans gliding
            across the ice in Florida Some cursive tongues or calligraphy made
of pure value the mood descending like soft rains in the tropics
            Every day is the dream of the desiccated Virgin Mary's head
who hovers above my body to mock the lush plants, the megaflora,
            to capture the line vanishing, the threshold vanishing, the apartment

vanishing, the vanished rent, to connect one vanishing point
            with another, how deeply one delves
into each side of the moment, how deeply the sentence
            turns into the café, the spirit world, a loud, drunken
discussion about politics or the aversion to certain
            foods, farewell, material I have plunged into it
            and the spirit world splashes around my form so how
can I resist the demons who insist I seem to be so much
            their semblance? The red walls of ice
lasted about an hour falling from the sky my son said, "That is
            weird. I have never seen that before." It is the end of
the pterosaurs, the end of machines, the end of marching
            bands and particle accelerators, it is the end of Diet
Coke, the end of chai tea, or Darjeeling and the lavender
            calming aromatherapy mist (for room and body)

Day is already what's in the wake of the irretrievable
            and for what, Horatio? Cones, pyramids, squares, bricks
of pills, the sunset breaking harsher and, in more elegiac
            tones, in crude relief like monotone

set against monotone or the obscene silk dresses
    flowing in the sugar-scented air that I wore
in Paris with my cousins eating lemon ice cream
    along the banks of the Seine you were already crashing
straight into my history of days swelling like a bad book
    thrown into dirty water and you knew it even though
it was smudged like the dream of carbon breaking into
    fossils, ideology and the smell of fat roots in the forest

The relief is so transient
    Get me out of here! But I felt faint or weak
or without the will or without hope
    because beauty does this to her sufferers
making a kind of lucid Maserati of the heavens
    The mock-heroic event horizon Maybe I'm the ruthless
one, the bad character in one of those novels by your bedside,
    the one who lies, cheats and steals but there's no way to know
for sure honey when you're given so little
    of the plot and all the other
characters are probably very seedy but stay silent (at least for now)
    as if we are all in the middle of a large body
of signals, a silence of aqua that has these high
    pitched sounds like metallic birds perforating in rings of cloud

We could be sitting in a coffee shop drinking tea and holding back
    our life stories Each history a long stay in the spiral staircase
of libraries and burnt gardens and I can't imagine why anyone
    would feel the desire to hurt a woman
who thinks about suicide every day
    But hey the lines are drawn and this oblong lake
is much more than an acquaintance
    Maybe the way pain in public is so
demonstrative and humiliating and also
    so affectionate, a giving that turns our cells

into something more than mere technology so that there's only
          ever some superficial layer of the epithetical light

I like the feeling of not crying
          but still wanting to
It's like prolonging the orgasm
          Some tantric impulse to the comets
Or maybe better to burn some incense because it is Saturday
          and the house is cool, calm and quiet like a plant
I like the build-up, the way it's like a short story or maybe
          short stories are like the breasts when they are hard
and full of milk and the baby is never gentle with what he wants
          and the sore nipple is also not gentle
with her giving I don't understand how anyone could
          have abandoned you, much less your mother and for what?
To have made you this creature forever stalking
          the evil light of a pool of blood fixating on the ring of flowers
at the bottom as if that ring could bring you back your mother
          or any narrative that made sense

One may scroll endlessly through a picture gallery of flowers:
          anemone, autumn joy, allium and to imagine that
there are twenty-five other letters of these ready to be planted,
          apple blossoms or azalea, and none of this you recognize
the Virgin Mary's desiccated, sepia-toned
          eyes floating so close to you trying to find water
so plants might bloom into the lush forms of volition,
          the complete face of compassion we must feel for our enemies
which is why I don't even understand why anyone would
          abandon anyone in our cold pastoral of rain, dirt, art, the stage set
of the Anthropocene gets all shot up like a gas station
          the way we watched Martha, Andy's mom on TV "And I looked down
and I realized it was his liver" and Andy and I laughed
          at the way his mother said this but how awful is it really, a trained nurse,

just getting some gas and coffee and then the whole
        thing descends into a wet liver on the horrible tiles
of a CONOCO station in New Orleans, so now I wonder

about Jason, the geologist, who kept threatening
        to kill himself and no one cared
until he went to Billings for work and got black-
        out drunk and shot a woman for no
reason he said, "Look at what you made me do!"
        which is what they all say "From Florida, he had few ties
to the Billings area" "Some things
        have no reason and that's why they are so hard
to understand" "How did you get away?"
        "I can't say for sure" "It's kind of a blur"
"I endured it" "I gave him what he wanted"
        "I was very afraid" "I knew he could kill"
"I promised that he would get something later"
        Because every story from the South
has to end with some theft, lies and betrayal
        and if it's a romance like I'm sure this one is
even though it is unthinkable to say so
        the moon will take the shape
of the face of that disaster
        looking back on itself in disbelief

Spring Dirge

I can't separate poetry
    from my life as a poet.
      If that means loving you past devastation,
         so be it. If that means fucking
      you past devastation. So be it.

They say the revolutionary objective
    is to smash history but I want
to smash the mirrors
    of history, the reality.

I don't want to kill myself.
    I want to kill the reification
      of my flesh, my flesh on the market
        hanging off hooks
  like the sides of animals,
    dangling and cold. Maybe
this is a pathological
    desire, a desire flowering
and borne of spring
      and maybe like
        the spring, wavering
inside her new water,
    she will leave us, for what use
is it to kill the dead?

But it is spring right here
    at this moment which is the only
spring the world has ever known
    and the only one
  that is important
  right now.

Loving you is not reasonable.
          Moreover, it is dangerous.
And even more than that there are so many of you
       just like those mirrors inside my body
            against my body on top of you
telling me that I'm not really you
       but I am you and you know it.

My poetry is so unsentimental.
          This is due to the brutish
way I was raised. It made my eyes
bluer, my senses keen
    like an animal intent
to survive the landscape
    of late capital. My poetry
         is opposed to the world;
it is a performance against
      ideology and honor
         and the nation state
and the mask I wear
is the performance is the mirror
       that I smash again and again.
Some people call it self-destructiveness
            but I call it love, statelessness,
       the anarchy of a flood of flowers.

Fuck honor. My poetry
          is a shield against the crisis of honor
and I invite all of you to fight
       on this side of that shield
which is the side of love and reckoning
       and on the other side is an ocean
of technology, ignorance
and fascist despair.

There is no honor
    defending the nation state.
There is no honor
    policing the nation state.
There is no honor
    in the patriarchy but it doesn't matter
anyway because fuck honor
and the way we will fuck honor
    is by making something so vulnerable
it will breathe in this spring air
and breathe out some
    tender fire like a dragon.

Maybe there is
    honor right here
in bed with you, in the sheer rebellion
    of ransacking Eros himself, that con
man who draws
me to you. I have dragged him through
    the drenched meadows
of April and May,
    dragged him through
that blue landscape
    in some humiliating display.
    Now that he has known love,
what will he do?

And afterwards, when it rains and rains
    and the city unfolds
like an apron or love letter or terrorism,
    I promise I will be with you
        whether you believe
these words or not.

A Poem for Criminals and Construction Workers

In the lush arboretum, Denali of dirges, denials, in the porcelain
    latticework of our architecture, lined with prissy sonnets and lace,
in the ankle bracelet monitors of the whore-lined chase, like pure luminescence,
        we went dancing (sort of), in the plain but packed and jagged angles of the
        day,
so my first question, which I will, in due time, rescind, is what is it that
        you see in me, but this is suddenly so obviously the wrong
question because it preserves a distance, a bas-relief like a bouquet of liars
        cuddling up to the conspiracy of a train of corruptible afterthought,
and also betrays a system of inflated self-congratulations,
        noteworthy for its lack, lack of what, exactly? Lack of conviction,
of impulse drawn from the dire weight of remote tangibles.

The criminal and her straightforward mode of behavior and speech,
        to hide, as it were, in plain sight, hanging out by the gaudy fountains,
dotted with statues, perfumed apricot and foaming crystalline parables,
        historic as shards of men laughably shiny. We do not know what it is
about their bodies that look so uncannily like their respective lack of interiority
        (to paraphrase a friend), as in a song you know is crappy,
bouncing down the lonely, wood-paneled hallway,
        but its beauty possesses you and strings you along the white collar
    of cognitive dissonance, and the only hope is to snap back,
        not to reality exactly, but to some former version

of understanding you had in your apprenticeship and somewhere hidden in those
        copious notes, a clue, so arch and detailed, the equations are flowers
    blooming into instances of rot, you could have been tested
on the entire opus and would have gotten an A+
    so easily, but rebelling against the privatized flesh like a plant, growing
the wrong direction, towards the seed instead of sky, sick with money,
and provisional explanations for blah blah blah I'm not listening,
        inequality, there ended up being a kinship

with either what, deep down, you are, or alternately, what you
        could be, the criminality, what we would have called,
in a former era, "wasted," which is what you did, isn't it,
        wasting the sun—that Riviera, wasting a few vines of privilege
        on sylvan notions of pride, or the even more perverse
notions of familial luck, as if that would amount to anything but loss,
        sudden and teetering like a wilted top, on even more loss,
            but it does not matter, the accent slowly flailing like a light ash downward,
                the way one cannot see any one living thing grow,
            but so suddenly, it is dead, and how did this happen without
        our noticing, how did the language bend away
from the spring-inflected window, when it should have
    bent toward the day, toward the open hand of luxurious opportunity,
    because, at heart, the criminality you feel isn't any different
        from what you already know, the barely
recognizable chalkboard glyphs of the previous class:

"detection" "malfeasance" "risk factors
        for deviance" "good
                for nothing" "malingering" "loser"
                "lost" She was lost.
                Rimbaud, as a teen, was detained
                    for roaming. She had been
                lost a long time.
                        Losing my
                            religion. Rimbaud always
                                made his way back
                                to his mom.
                    That fucking loser.
                    What a loser.
                        Loser.
                            Lost.

The worthlessness of this lesson in community policing,
        the class taught before mine, how I want to scream, "But this is
all wrong!" the desks like wind chimes, a trance devoted exclusively
to conglomerating business, the ease with which
        ordinary people talk about accumulating wealth
and keeping people out and keeping up nationalism
        like mowing one's lawn and planting coordinated,
    obedient flowers in wooden boxes, as if one's life
    were simply waiting for the right flag to settle quietly over one's grave.

    How triumphant! To shout, "But this is all wrong!" to no one,
        to the quivering South Georgia field, drenched in its own
    acute madness, and also lonely, those centuries steeped
        in overwhelming resentment and violence, so they must feel
            incredibly lonely too but what do I care
            about the nuanced feelings of the victors?

At the board, words like keys to a prison, where women
    pose in their prison yoga class, or confess this or that in their prison
        AA meetings, a revolving lapse
        of judgment, a few pills, some weed, a bad
            check, and the whole story
            turns into juggling the bureaucracy of time—time in,
    time out, time left, time served, time spent,
        and all the while like cafeteria food, the grades
of meats get worse, the quality so low it is hard to call it "food,"
    maybe just calories, counted out meticulously by state workers,
        doled out by a corporation which also serves food
            at the county fairs, alongside the fattest
                orange pumpkins and antibiotic goats
            and at what point in the story
                do I bring up that I married a construction,

I wed a grid, an arrangement, a system
　　of phonemes layered like blushing scraps, and inside
　　　　the resilient yet contradictory night, the sad, corporeal palm trees,
　　　　　　swaying like a robed chorus,
　　　　a Miami of waves gushing up against the white lifeguard stands,
　　　　　　the art deco cinema of shell, heat, a tropic of violence,
　　　　　　　where we discussed the terrors, qualities, successes and failures
　　　　　　of our incorporated makers, and how we made our way
　　　　　　　　with resolve, without much
　　　　　　　to hang on to, billowing out like a cheap sheet
　　　　　　into the blinking atmosphere, the way two people, out
　　　　　　　of nowhere, reach for each other,

　　or commiserate on the relative merits
　　　　of the ornithology program at Cornell University,
　　　but this, of course, is a mask, a gorgeous cover
　for class, as if the mere knowledge of a tiny fact
　　　　is the touchstone, the passcode, a marker of knowing
　　　　　　who you are, "But this is all wrong!"
　　　　the plasma of subjectivity revolving
　like a ballerina, all that weight, pressure
　and formulated beauty converging
　　　　on a tiny satin point at the tip of her toe, a sand grain
　　　　　on our distilled matrix—glassy and prismatic.

A Lover's Discourse

My story is difficult; it is one of despair.
        Happy songs selling songs are not
            my weapon here.
      To dissect a year: Sing along
      rotten chimes
        gone wrong.
Write a comet, Aphrodite. Repair
       the subject. A note or two
     about love: I love the quasar! Her tentacles,
       her trance of blood in a city
          as she drinks. The street
           is a trace of lemons,
     a mud bath. Stars that break
    through their own
    demonology. Oppression like the phases
      of the peach: Moldy, tender, a pit, a grave.
Incomplete value. Temperamental. Estranged.
    I take off my lover's uniform.
                I call him "Uniform"; he's just
               some petty shopkeeper
              but I touch his chest hair,
        force myself to listen to his moronic pauses,
    his moronic reasoning. My story is difficult;
    it is one of despair. It is the inverse
       of a line of votives. Church mouse,
         it is the inverse of church squared.

    *

I like the way comets are just like, "Fuck you, whatever."
What's the matter? You don't seem to be happy.
I like the way they think. Their logic
is sound. It is granite.
I take for granted their clarity and I enjoy
the way they demystify some
essential affirmation of spunky
social media gurus.
I saw masses of people swarm
the glaciated brainchild
of doubt. Oh Uniform,
come hither, you bastard. You dumb
piece of the plural good. Some glittering stupidity
like the eyeball of a round lamb.
Come, my little comet. You baby doll.
Hi back. To your gorgeous desire
to suffer in realism.

*

Born of literature, berated by work.
Beaten down by the inflections of viability.
To my own philosophy, I am none!
Uniform's truck is gone.
Zero energy's the only wise thing I know:
to gather as undertaking, to undertake
as gathering. To be one's
own undertaker. These worn codes
refresh themselves by the moment
as bone. We break
through them if we cannot
afford to. I love you.
But not enough. Not yet and beyond some
limit where life is
what's reversed.

*

"The sun's magnetic field is poised to flip."
I speak to myself as my own
        horrified narrator; it's sick.
    Inside the ticking keyhole of language,
    you grip some corrupted verbs
and call it a day. Or a vase. Or hyperbole.
    Or a wage. Talking
  to yourself like ancient, brazen
    history. White page after
      white page, skin tone
            encased like a hard drive,
              information is what
                  it transplants.

    *

    The anxiety of losing
  the lover is a Bronze Age guise to remake
reality. A mask. Your remarks are clever.
    In other words, hell.

    *

Yet you dazzle me with your little piece of medieval flesh.
    When will you admit that I surmount
        your repetitive and myopic
        star work? The New Year
    exhumes some commonplace
          errors. One rule of thumb would be
that our story is ours that our love is ours
        that we keep our scrolls because we do not know
      anything other than an altar
        of syncope and endless

banalities. A lovely phrase like the skin
of a flayed shark. At times, I crave cheap
Chinese food so hard. Or the sea that
continues along its course of wrecks.
I look out my window and the stillness
of the rural scene
breaks my heart.

*

Devout as I am, the devouring's
stronger. A horrible ebb
within the phone's dreaded
contents. Secretions pulsate like various
forms of criminality. Text me or circulate
like intense visions of Mary
in palm trees or coral reefs.
Every so many seconds a woman is hit by a man
with direct tectonic rage. Geology
is some rough sadism I know
not what. Agony is property
but it is also agony. Vow to me, agony!
Declare your allegiance! (Or buy me a house.)

In the hotel, alone, I wait for jealousy
to return me to everything I know.
Some fucked-up figure will either fuck
me or become the background to
my intensely cold hands.

*

The terror of a breakdown is the background
of the History of Art. I am calm. Anxiety mounts.
Having lost him, I move closer to the comet's
deranged equipment. I situate myself inside
the overblown moment as if
I am the birthright of madness.
I enslave the bathtub. Doped up
lamps are stupid and I'm not okay.
I am my breakdown; I'm not okay.
Wrecking my life was the origin of love.
Read about the Hittites or Hitler.
Above, the sun
is a carved marble.

*

Oh Barthes, is there some triumphant dictionary,
some magic charm that will save
me from the rent ruin,
the wage ruin, the loan ruin,
the him ruin, the page ruin, the nerve ruin?
Maybe that dictionary wears hymns around her neck
and lives in the country
and is content with nothing
less than making a demonology
of the granular surface.

*

Maybe she keeps goats. Maybe her home
is in the sun where all the suicides
go for their little banquet of wine
and milk and trees? Maybe she knows
the passageway to the mountains? Perhaps she is a song

that can only please her enemies. Perhaps with one
glance she can slice through the agony
of property. Maybe she dances in a shell.
Maybe she wears no uniform at all.
Maybe she is really a skull. Or a pulse.
Maybe she smells like weeds on the seashore.

Further Problems with Pleasure

There must be some way to prolong the house.
I doubt I will ever use the word *plywood* in a poem
so there's no way I could build anything substantial. Anyone
got a razor I haven't shaved in over a year. I could write a hundred of these,
binge on free speech. "I am intensely attracted to you,"
he said a year later. There were monitors everywhere
and they streamed through the world like phantoms.
It induced a kind of paranoia in some but others
found comfort in it. Let me never be the one
who finds comfort in the sherbets of prison so that I can
kiss you and stay a love poet. There must
be some way to prolong the house.

A Song for Paperweights

To enter the room
of a thousand paper-
weights, one descends
  rapidly. And the more clarity
one has, the more rapidly
one descends. Each weight,
  its own descent
  into glass beehives
    that refract the reality
of every
    given
situation.

                    *

Goethe, as a boy, wore a coat
        of green wool
          with little gold frogs
      embossed on it
and at his side a miniature
        sword. If you read *Poetry*
and My Life,
Goethe sounds a little
        insane. How I admire
my sister's great disdain
        for hysteria.

                    *

I, however, readily
    descend into
the molten, millefiori
    of the seen. When I think
of Clare (a girl from
        high school)
        and her Facebook
updates: "You got a
new daddy. ARE YOU
COMPREHENDING
        L.A. HO with da husband? *LOAN
FORGIVENESS*.
        The MBA you working on at dat
IVY LEAGUE is *PAID* for.
        Orphans and MOM
paid for," I admire
    my sister's remove
        but don't
            have it in me.

        *

Why did Clare choose
    the wrong friends
in high school?
        All stockbrokers
and lawyers now. (God, they're
            beautiful to my dorkiness.)
        With the exception of my
sister (while disdaining!),
who is the devout one, the one
who loves the Lord
    and forgiveness (and all of that stuff
I know nothing about),

they were all
worthless, cruel.

                *

"It's free love until
        you have to wipe
a baby's ass," my friend says
    at dinner talking about
the possibilities
        of a free
love commune.

                *

If you give them enough time,
        the paperweights trail off
into what they can't trap, into
the streaked harmonium
        of what surrounds them—a lizard,
            a hat, marsh, wheat, the "oh"
                of a man falling asleep on
a train trip across New Brunswick (this is
the last time he will think
        of his daughter but how could
he know this being
caught inside glass),
seagull feather a little girl
        picks up on her way to school, the very
        eye of the beholder
as if the body could
measure something
            precisely
                long after
            it has escaped.

                    *

To trade seventeen
    lampwork glass
    beads for three slaves.

                    *

When we are inside this room
    of a thousand paperweights,
     are we the last
        painting of sorrow? Radiation
            and snow, the leopard jumps from its
                haunted number, from the thrilling
                    gold leaf and pale ivy
        borders of a fifteenth-century manuscript
into this patchwork narrative
            we are forced
            to call "landscape."

                    *

We trail off too,
    cobble
        together
what we can. Or late at night
    we doze off in front of the computer
        reading some meaningless
    comment on a webpage. "My man
        loves fettuccini
alfredo and oddly enough
    the Olive Garden is the place
to go for it."

Fun Clothes: A Gothic

Schizophrenic like suds in the afternoon, bubbles and bubbles of the glorious
prism, molds of forensic happenings, and you speak softly in a delectable armory,
    in feathers,
busts, bras not afraid of being impoverished, afraid, alas, that this disguise will
    morph
to human flesh, the underneath in chains that vibrate the invisible soundscape
of deposits, a debt the color of frog skin, how can he hold back the incredible lush
    device that is
the body, the last of the last, the one whose dressing room appears in the
    negative, a cold cloud, sound
of the funerary ocean, cobalt abyss beckoning like rain, like rain down the spine
    of beauty,
like loosening shivers, like oh this archaic mall, once the epicenter of commerce
    and crime,
and how now it's just opals of dwindling energy, a caveat for cowgirl boots w/
    Christian crosses stitched
all over them, a cache of zirconium encrusted socks, and the long, tan arms of the
    Lemon Girls,
whose promises you already know are lies, but you buy a few anyway, why? Just
    because
there's no reason not to, a parchment of brain matter, the guessing game, some
    pathetic
employee made of ham, some ham made of polyester, some polyester made of the
    light organs,
and still they built this mall on a plan of mild humiliation like meadowland that
    makes us feel
somehow inept when facing its triumphant posture of flower, water and seed,
    more the appendectomy,
the obligatory jog on a workday, see how the light gathers in these bent arcades, I
    have followed
you in decades past, your memory like Mother who took us to buy Guess jeans,
    the feeling

intense as light stored years back, confronted, denied, laughed about but it wasn't funny,

none of it was, and settling on junk, since that's what this is, multicolored, made from the laugh lines

of others, detached, touched, how I want you so much and how this shopping mall does

the trick, it always does, don't humiliate me though, I know I look ill, out of place and old

in this leotard, but still, I was compelled into it, catapulted into it, thrown into it

and I couldn't stop myself, couldn't resist it and when I touched it, like Eve who could not resist what

she would become, I thought it would transform me like something deep within Ovid, or that inside my

soul I was indeed Ovid, and that if only I put on the leotard, I would become Ovid

again and again and you would want me back, see, so it made a kind of sense,

the kind of sense a muse makes when she says the word Givenchy, I could become that, right?

or something like Givenchy, better even, the breasts more solid with a lineage a straight line from

the golden age of all breasts, Givenchy, Italian, French, located in the place where

you don't have to work, where there's no loneliness, Givenchy, the frilly island, Givenchy, the Greek,

How I want you, Givenchy, to bleed your melancholic streaks of song into my song,

you are an owl to me, you are the Song of Songs, Givenchy, Gestapo, Givenchy,

and I know you know how to teach me to remember how much nothing transforms,

and how you said there is beauty in the emerald, and how you claimed it was enough but it was not

enough for me, and then you made me feel guilty for wanting more from you, and then you said, I can't

give you anything but beauty, the dynamics of the trend, all I can give you, Sandra, is this,

this decrepit shopping mall with a sad car parked inside of it, the knotted terror of
  the paycheck,
that's what you said you could offer, bad value like bad love, and I bought into it
  because I was
desperate, not for you, but for that anxiety to leave my body, to make its final exit,

I do not fear death, Givenchy, I fear you will overtake the sublime knowledge of
  Poetry
and Nature so I must beat you back to powder, beat you out of my mind and body
like a power structure, a war on war, a breakdown of the light your mall
  constructed,
and a breakdown of the mall in the mind that you have constructed, and a
  breakdown
of the neuron mess that we have constructed out of the sad bits of culture, cloth,
and human longing with your opulent maison, and one by one we will burn your
  maisons,
and the websites of your maisons and your models and your actress-models
and your poet-models and your novelist-models and your great conceptual artist-
  models
and there will be nothing left of you, you will be out in the cold when the mall is
  not burned
but gone, wiped out, no trace left of it for miles and miles around,
nothing left to transform into or out of, so I walked out of the mall into the
  glaring
and relentless prison of the present and I realized I was the fool, a victim of false
  hope
and how even that epiphany is so dull, I'm embarrassed, and when I walked out
  of the mall,
I realized, but hell, I realized nothing, I go home not Ovid but me, a sandstorm,
I go home me and not you and not me and you and not Ovid and me and you just
  me
and my leotard, so out of touch with reality, so out of style already, that nature
  mocks it
immediately, and there's nothing the moon or sun or stars can tell me tonight to
  make it better.

Our Lady of Perpetual Help

All this magic against death
Live the light in August that's it
Look at the way the leaves tint themselves for autumn
    The yellow ribbed frog is extinct as of 12/1/2013
I was an amphibian creeping like the Bible
Something incandescent or comely but
my eyes can't dissect your eyes like an electric rabbit
    named Paul Revere
      I will die with a glass heart in my hand
      I will die with a glass heart in my hand
You need to repeat after me
This is Mississippi
      The moon is dusted terrible

You learned how to spell me in school terrible
    You need to mark every place Faulkner was racist
and rewrite the novel as erasure
If you're good man, you'll rewrite the moon
and then we will fall for each other backwards
   which is our birthright
Which is the soft land and her animals
   when nature mellows like a porous fruit

As you become a character enclosed in my grammar,
    you become an object I'm ashamed
    The yellow frogs are gone did you see them parting?
Things grow long and unrecognizable
Love is recognized as an archaic structure
    of scribbles, vines, buttresses, spires
    conspiracy theories, weak as gas station coffee

You see six nuns in South Alabama moving
towards a gas station named Brittney
like a prehistoric herd in the mauve twilight
They have gone down the War on Terror
        Memorial Highway in their big bus vroom vroom
They are not right Not of our century
They are the cryptic language of the kill
        They are not who they pretend to be
One is pregnant under her habit
        One thinks she ought not to touch that
One buys a Diet Dr. Pepper and Twizzlers

They go down the highway, a sparkling acid trip
    They are psychedelic and crazed as lions crave energy,
their eyes revolving like enervated shadows
in the painted murals of their thinking
    They are snorkeling inside the waters of death
They are not the gentle motion of waves
but rather the cold deaths of rivers and crosses
  burdened with poison
        They are the death
of orgiastic chimneys, soot
        and the frail air that surrounds it
as the flesh surrounds the heart
    and is also the heart

They go down the highway on God
        I want you to say this, Mississippi   6 miles
        I want you to love terror, Alabama   10 miles
I want you to place yourself on the interior
        of this spiked gothic, Mississippi   15 miles
I want you to listen in and tell me
        you love me, Mississippi   85 miles
I will squeeze it out of you like a glass heart

thrown into parts of the earth
      you don't want to see, Mississippi   132 miles
I will die with a glass heart in my hand
as if it's a diamond encrusted scepter I know it
     I am the queen of this disaster
I can feel it deep inside me

This is a torch
        This is a door
This is a tree
        This a gun
This is a nun
        This is a pregnant nun
This is none
        This is the baby inside the nun
This here is Baby None
        Say hello to None Hi None
This ain't Baby None No
        Say Bye to Baby None No Bye None
Inside the War on Terror Memorial
        Highway is Family None
driving to nothin'
None of it I've said before
        Nothing has gone down
this highway except deer
        and the desolate streaks of None
This is a place of weeping things
     where the world has wept
    and wept and no one has come

No Father None   No Mother None
No Baby None Comes   No Sister
None Comes No Brother None Comes
No One   like None

It's that kind of place
       You've never seen it before
       It's blind to everything, everyone
Halfway extinguished, halfway extinct

Never mind the gas station or the girl who barfed
             in the van of Christmas tinsel
or the nuns who have dissolved
       into the South Alabama mist
No one sees them except us and that
       is why we love each other

This is my life
I don't want it I do
     These are the frogs I don't want them I do
These are the nuns I don't want them

I do no more I do
I do know more   I know I do none
I do no more   none I know I do
I do to you

Further Problems with Pleasure

Sometimes I wonder what the novel would have looked
like if instead of plots its characters had bodies
—Chris Nealon

I love to sit by this lake midmorning
                              when I'm slightly hungover.
I love the way the water moves
                              everything to the west, pulls
the birds, tampons, pills, condoms,
                              cups with it. Cosmopolitan
vortex. A century of Black Fridays
                              splashes up to its disgusting
shores. Wondering how much of life is
                              spent getting fucked, or fucking,
getting fucked over or just being
                              a fucker. Maybe some want
a grand narrative instead of this
                              instantaneous flesh flash mob
bullshit but I can't help loving
                              the way you want me
to suck your dick. Why can't sheer
                              beauty kill this century
the way it kills me? All the poets write
                              poems titled "Dear So and So"
but I retaliate and instead sit right
                              here in the middle of this lake.

The Woman with the Foreign Accent

When I ask her where
she is originally from
she says, "Vermont."
"Vermont?" I ask.
"Yes, Vermont," she says folding each
dinner napkin into a swan and letting
each one slip from her hands as if
letting slip vowels or consonants,
freeing them from a conquered language,
loosening them like feathers
from the borders, county lines,
dotted shapes of the interstate, removed,
from the ambulance siren
of the minor tongue, which,
in its opulence, must needlessly
justify itself over and over.

I think of my mother who says
to any passerby very proudly,
"I'm from France," and I ask my friend
why the woman with the foreign accent
lies about her accent since my mother never lies
about being French,
and my friend says, flatly,
"Because France is cool."

What if the woman
with the foreign accent
comes from a family of Nazis and has spent
her whole life keeping her
family's dark secret?

Or what if her father
is a monster and she decided
early on that she would
leave her mother tongue, move
to America, spend summers
on a motorcycle driving through
New England, stopping on
the way to Vermont or Maine
at the occasional bed and breakfast
but also deciding to never, ever
get too emotionally close
to anyone she meets?

Everywhere in the hinterlands,
the countryside quakes
with regret or astonishment. The trains
and cows, the only remnants of collusion.
And when you really think about it,
everyone, everywhere,
has an accent
when they go
somewhere else.
Everyone, that is, except babies.

Vermont? But, Vermont what?
Or what if the woman with the foreign accent
is a double agent? Or do double
agents even have
foreign accents? Or diplomats?
What if she's the woman
who gave the "okay"
for the president of Poland's plane
to be shot down? What if she's the one
who pushed the red button

that sent an alarm so that
everyone at the factory
where they make toy trains
was suddenly instructed to leave
due to the chemical spill?
Is this how the community is spared?
Is this how the circles
of friendship tighten
into merry-go-rounds of gossip,
channels and pools of vague paranoia?

It was late in the evening and my
friends and I sat on the porch steps
drinking root beer and eating
crackers while the plump deer
of the environs chewed
blackberries. The sea,
in the background, did whatever
it does, suspiciously.

Beyond some
fence, another fence, and beyond
that fence, another fence, and perhaps
a bit farther out, something out
of nowhere lands on a house
and the explosion ripples outward
from the house to the watery village.

"Who, in the end,
stole the ping pong equipment?"
I asked my friends between crackers
but everyone shrugged
and, as a shorthand to all needlessly
tangled plots, the mystery is never solved

and word never does come back to us
from the village, except for the word
carnage, which the woman
with the foreign accent pronounces
"car-nich" but difficult to pay
attention to, considering tube tops
and violet leggings are back
in style and never mind
the complex drop-off
pick-up schedule of my children.

　　　Let the gentle pastel rains
of Florida enable ways for us to feel
more deeply about homes, bodies,
and set them against the whorish intrigue
of book burning, the beloved
hashtags that bring us right to
the pinpoint morgue of the sun.
One must have a mind
of something. Not winter, exactly,
but something.

　　　I began to question
why the woman with the foreign accent
suddenly bloomed like minnows
enclosed in a globe of water, the habitat
which one could buy on the internet,
complete, a perfected love
insulated from the world around it,
devoid of class structure, of any structure
at all, in fact, taken out
of the small cardboard box
and placed on the bamboo

countertop of a sushi bar
in Seattle so the customers
don't notice the minnows
immediately, but rather they see
an indistinct globe of water, with nothing
inside it except a bit of swaying
miniature seaweed, until midway
through dinner when, half drunk on sake
and full of salmon and rice—but this is when
it all comes to me—

I even put down my phone
for a second, savoring
the epiphany. I just *know*.
When the deer charged at me, I stepped out
of the way like a professional
and it ran straight
into the saltwater night.

I said goodbye to my friends
on the porch, went into the house,
walked over piles library books,
my psyche encrusted
with wild lamentation, ridiculous
emotional excess,
obscene sentimentality.

The ping pong equipment,
neat in its white, netted bag,
sat on the kitchen table, next to
a ceramic vase of plastic lilies,
autumn-colored the way a season
closes in on you, and then you look up

from the screen and it is already
gone and it felt as if, all along,
everyone was in on it,
as if the equipment
never disappeared.

The Baudelaire Variations

1. Destruction

There's a demon on the Oregon coast whose pale form
        swims towards me but I am an avalanche of air;
my desire is brutish—I can't couple with anyone.

        Sometimes art takes the form of the seduction of women
    or I give women some sort of pretext to account
for myself and my art which is, in itself, a hideous form.

Sister, why do you think I should look toward God?
        I'm tired; I'm in the middle of some
feast of tiredness and it's just the Sahara Desert here
            and will be forever.

You throw sand in my eyes to confuse me and I cry,
        "Demon, leave me alone! Don't open
the door to this stupid destruction."

2. A Martyr

In the middle of a pool of falcons, I am voluptuous
      but lame. And marbles. And more
marbles on the table. I wear a rose
      dress, perfumed with lament.

In this room, I have hurt myself so I become
      dangerous, fatal and even the mourner's bouquet
      cannot save my wolf head.

I am a cadaver, but what do I do with it?
      I am dead labor, but what do I do with it?
It's like having blood but no prey.

My visions are pale gold shadows
      over my eyes which make my head just ache
and ache like some sort of historic idiot.

When night falls, I rest on this table
      and think about the white skin of revulsion.
Oh on this bed, I am the secretary
      of abandonment. A rosary and coins

of gold and the leg, the damned blue leg!—
      there can be no diamond skulls
      in the world after all.

I am the portrait of my own provocations
      and what strange feelings of strangeness
      I have felt on this table.

Oh I am elegant! But irritated.
    Everyone should desire me.
Respond to me, Felix. Once you called me "deranged"
      and "impure" but I am the world
      and I am that strange creature

inside of you, this mysterious
    table, hand and the constant
  eyeball of death.

3. Eros and the Skull

Diamond inflected skull, you are not
          humanity. Whatever profane emotions
you feel are an affront

    to your blond architecture,
now in ruins, the stone mouths of lions,
      also in ruins. Your moment in the world
is over like a gargoyle crushed
      into a fine powder and used to purify the face
        of a lonely woman.
                And in that original ether, your globe
takes out its dead, game hand
        as if it is king here.

I crave some ridiculous and frail end, Brother,
      that only a stratosphere
        of endlessness could consume.

    So, if you are the Monster Assassin, this time
      show your face
        in my gray blood.

4. The Albatross

A lot of times, I think things are really funny, Felix.
Take for example, the albatross, that vast bird of the ocean.
Every time he goes on a trip, his native land
glistens and I ride far on the surfaces of his love.

You can't dispose of that bird, nor can you compose
the haunted rose light around his brutal white tongue.
Leave me alone, Felix. Leave me to my place
on this coast of crystals and sea foam.

Bad, bad trip. I'm talking about these drugs
and that beautiful bird, so comic and light
in the gay air. I want to drink with him all night until
he engulfs every coast in his distant clouds.

Poets are the princesses of the nude and the dark.
I hate my temper and all I seem to have left in my exile
is this dumb laughter bouncing inside the sun of a million hues—
Oh how the crowd beats down on giants.

5. Jewels

The most expensive thing in the world, dear Felix, is nudity.
And nudity knows my heart is a huge, beating sonorous jewel.
Inside my body, therefore, is something rich,
something happy and full of the slaves of death.

When I dance, something brutal happens. The brilliant world
of metals and stones disappears into my dreaming limbs
and because I love fire, things catch on fire,
and then those things, Felix, they pour out light.

She was asleep on the sofa, so I watched her with love.
I didn't want to see her smile or frown—just sleep, profound
and soft as the sea; this is how she came to me in dreams.

Her eyes fixed on mine, like a tiger, resigned to her fate,
and inside the vague, hot air of the room something new appeared,
a metamorphosis of sorts, her arms, her legs, they took the reins,
as if all along she had something clairvoyant about her.

Something ancient and calm, an agent of evil
was sent to trouble my sleep, my soul, and derange
those rocks and crystals, so I couldn't be calm
or solitary when that angel was around me.

In that sleep, I swear I saw a new design, the poles,
the antipoles of the earth—drunk, busted, resigned
and that anarchy made me feel huge and superb.

But lamps die. And in the room where she slept, there was only
a little light left, a little incense, inundated in song and blood
like a jewel at the bottom of a cup, a little color
unsteady as the amber shadows.

6. The Possessed

The sun converts into a gauzy moon,
the moon of my life that is! All shadow, all fumes—
I'm so fucking exhausted, Felix.

And yet I love you! And if you want today,
like an eclipse of sorts, like a phenomenon,
we can enter our madness again, enter the tomb
of the surging crowd and it will be good.

Look at your eyes, those chandeliers.
Look at mine, my brother. I'm compelled by
some overwhelming lust, some morbid, thrilling pleasure.

Black night. Red dawn. You can be
whatever you want me to be. There's not a fiber
in my body that doesn't cry for you,
cry—*Oh my dear Satan, je t'adore!*

7. Exotic Perfume

When my two eyes close on a warm autumn night, I sweat
    the smell of your hot skin, and I feel the blazing rivulets
of happiness that fuel the inferno of the monotonous sun.

We have come to this lazy island together, Felix,
where nature offers shivering trees with shivering red fruit,
  cold as an ancient orgy. This place where the men
are thin and vigorous and the women are fresh and sassy like sin.

My god, this climate, it charms me but also
     makes me so very tired, all that vague marine—
just piles and piles of sea on sea like corpses,
       blue on obscene blue endlessly.

What the fuck do I know about what is perfumed?
Felix, I know nothing about what is green.
      Something lush circles the air above us.
   It's a soul, I'm sure of it. Or some sort of screen.

8. I Love Wine!

Today, omg, I'm just so spaced out and splendid
        as I walk this earth without death, without an apron,
without being a wife and so my queer heart transforms into the nostrils of a
        winter
        workhorse whose exhalation breaks through the iced tulip sky.

Why does everyone want to torture me?
        All people care about are calendars, clocks, wallets
to cut off and time the flesh; Well, I can't take it!

So here *ich bin*, unbalanced and delirious, here *je suis*,
        tapping into some long forgotten intelligence—

Oh Felix, let's go to the Oregon coast
        and relax inside the boxed wine paradise of our dreams.

9. Allegory

She's beautiful and rich and runs a publishing empire
so even her most miniscule thought is the color of corpse champagne
and those little devils in her hair, all dead factory workers,
don't complain when she takes down that quartz waterfall at night
for they will live pinned forever in her dragonfly-shaped barrettes.
When she is naked, those poor monsters flow from her hands
and say, very weakly, in unison, "Oh Madame Deluxe, you can't feel the pleasures
      of hell
that we feel!" But that is total bullshit. When she looks into the mirror,
the face of her own death is simply majestic and everybody knows it.

10. Metamorphosis of the Vampire

You know the kind I'm talking about: a sort of snake lady,
all bruises and torqued flesh dancing
in a Montana river with trout, beer cans and flies.
Pregnant with science, music, mud and fronds,
her conscience has the tarnished, antique quality
of a century of sin.

           It makes me laugh to think that she's
           a woman who cannot die and, for eternity, must
           speak, eat and sleep like a babbling infant.

11. Damned Ladies

I shout, "Get your asses off the couch!"
    and they turn to me, all the damned ladies of my past,
as if their eyes, put together, are the gray, dilapidated horizon
    just above the sea. They could care less
about my reproaches, those soft sponges.

I think, Felix, that those sisters are in cahoots!
    Yes, they have marched from the grave just
    to wash my mouth out with their blood.
In their hands, I see the resins of the past

and they will not move from the Bacchus-like sediment
    of their flesh. But, Felix, listen. They are not venomous
    those cow snails, those pillows,
    nor are they my true tormentors.

The gigantic reality of their contemptuous spirits
    stretches infinitely like a gauze cloud before
my imagination. Oh Felix, I am full of my own
    long, lame, black satin tears
which are satyrs that morph to fill the sky

like fruit bats and who could contain even
    the faintest soul in this day and age?
And as I turn my attention back

to those poor, poor, unmovable sisters, sages,
    tramps, cows, breasts, anemones, virgins,
  blobs, amoebas, cavities, the sea's holes,
the salt, the sand dunes—

I love them with the plainness of this speech
    and I beg them to fill my urn
with the dust of their empty hearts.

12. The Fountain of Blood

Sometimes I want you to bite my neck hard
and let the blood flow down in a fountain, the liquid, rhythmic
and murmuring and eventually I want that blood to hit the little rocks
of your testicles below my wet mouth. When I leave you, I hate

to walk across the city, still deep in my tight, circular orgasm,
and I don't want to transform that moment into something we
must call "nature" which is only a warzone of buildings, work,
street corners, pigeons, Styrofoam trays and concrete.

Darling, one cannot color nature red. Therefore, I demand
that you sleep with me every night and pour wine
over my nipples and after you cum, I want you to open

your eyes, every fucking night, to this new century:
Don't you see? It will always be the very last time, eternally, one last time,
and I want you to say, "Felix, cruel girl, love is not for you."

13. Voyage to Cythera

My heart is like a bird going on a sea voyage to find utter joy,
the way an anxious and anemic adolescent
pins a corsage through the paper nipple of his warped drawing
of a young, freckled nude. And just like this,
I, myself, radiate that sun-filled madness.

So I must ask you, Felix, as we approach
the island Cythera together on our funky canoe,
why, if I feel so light and airy, is Cythera so dismal?

As we paddle closer to the shore, the salt-
encrusted crows, sonic warnings, caw and caw,
and as I dip my bare feet into the weepy waters
and pull our boat to shore I hear, from the distant
center of the island, the mud-caked
yodeling of ancient men and women.

Walking toward the center of Cythera,
down its one path, whose dust chokes me,
I see a sad procession of headless lovers,
a few of them beating tattered tambourines.

As the music grows more intense,
I find a scraggly pine tree to hide behind . . . and just in time!
For behold these ghosts and their queen, Aphrodite,
that terrible beauty with her obsessed face,
who leads the procession towards the town square.
Behold the ghosts who circle before her.
If you have never seen a procession

of ghosts kneeling before their queen,
then you have lived a life without trouble.

In a sudden state of horror, I turned back
and, Felix, brother, guide, companion, father,
mother, sister, Virgil, everything—you were gone!
Alone here? Could this be true? To suffer
the terror of abandonment? How shall I return
to Oberlin, Ohio, to my basement
where I keep the drawings
of Petula Smith, that innocent high school girl I love?
For this is not an island of dreams
but rather an island of suffocating nectars that
drip from overgrown, deranged flowers.

I was holding onto a branch of the pine
and it broke and the noise of the crack
caught the queen's attention. She looked at
me and I could saw her eyes were
two endless black holes.

She began to walk toward me and the blood
in my body spilled into the holes
that were her eyes and in that moment
I realized that I was Cythera's
one corpse, Aphrodite's victim hanging
upside down from a half-dead tree.

I couldn't even taste the vomit in my mouth
as the ghosts surrounded me but I forced myself to look
at the dirt of the earth which was now beyond
the sky when the soft scent of carnations and salt
grew tighter around my neck while Aphrodite, like a bird,
whispered into my dead ear, "The only thing
I ever wanted was to share my island with you."

14. The Sick Muse

My poor, poor, sick muse, hello. What are you doing today?
      Your creamy eyes, all purple with nocturnal visions,
I see you reflected in every tint of the world—all of it—
      The madness, the horror, the cold taciturn hell of it.

I can't succumb to you so quickly, but all my verse
      pours so easily into the rose love of your urns.
I could try to hide it, but the depth is despotic,
      and all I really care to do is float on your rhythmic waves.

I don't know how to be healthy, Felix,
      don't know that particular exhalation, and I think of you
so deeply, so furiously, all the time.
      It's a sickness, but I want it.

Come with me, let's count out these antique syllables
      while we can for we are the mothers of our own songs.
      Phoebus and the fantastic Pan, they have built
      their houses out of us with their mythological blood.

15. Eternity

The demon in the hot, hot chamber
    came to see me in my hot, hot chamber
and I lost everything, everything
    because he claimed he was my savior.

Everything is beautiful! Everything!
        And I am beauty's lost enchantment,
composed of all the flesh's charms.

What is the softest thing in the world, Felix?
    It is my penis; it is my soul and it is
    abhorrent and nothing will stop it.

I don't want you to ravish me; I don't
    want you to ignore me either or
  seduce me. I just want you to
    consume me in the way that
the old masters did since harmony

    is too exquisite and governs everything,
like the O in every metamorphosis
    where some mystical One
  hails music, hails perfume like a cunt.

16. This Stuff Is Poison and It's Gonna Fuck Up My Shit

The wine says the world is either bourgeois or already dead,
but by some luxurious miracle, I am still here, having emerged once again from
that red vapor. And like the sleeping sun, I am the noble one.

But there are worse drugs, Felix. There are drugs long and illuminated,
and born of complete enmity and they stalk us the way time
does, boom boom with its mean fist; it's music but it's also catastrophic.

All these poisons, where do they go? Where do they position
themselves in the eyes, where in the soul? I just don't know.
I don't want to be their terrible prodigy, their human weight,
their fleshy matter, inside the vertigo they spin, don't want to be
their sad, spinning pawn in the poisoned river of death.

My Sexuality Is "Victim of Capitalism"

My gender is pink jeans. My sexuality is longing
and taking that longing
down the long, red dawn
spread like a fan
across the bed. I don't think
I'm gay. I don't think I'm straight.
I think I'm going to change into my pussy
is always wet these days as if Eros
itself had taken up permanent residence
in the stupid garage of my body.

My pussy doesn't believe
in ecological collapse or
trees or the sunset; it doesn't believe in the moors,
the Brontës, the heart
or the landscape opening and closing
like a fist. It can't resist. It just keeps going
going like a machine
placing its bets like an idiot
on a rigged game.

I've made a few babies.
I built them from some cross between
revolution and youth like a girl
who has the word *fate* tattooed
on her forearm because she can't
stand anything and the act
denotes her lack of intelligence
which is sad but real.

Yesterday, at a birthday dinner
someone was talking about Rumi,
some fable that involved a lion
and a woman. Something abstract was stacked
on seven Korans. Maybe it was Eros or
love or the sun. I can't remember.

But something about the story
moved my flesh like light against
the crescent moon
and I wondered, Alex, if you too wanted
to make a spirit
out of this nothingness,
an ash spirit, trash everywhere trash,
and fling it across the hotel
window to make reality
a scene before us.

To the Mother of the Setting Day

The absence of sadness may create bitterness. I will give any goddess
who makes her way through this cheap ass apartment a free
pair of Minnie Mouse embossed baby socks. I was up all night
      rearranging the water
that poured from six clear
     opals and, in the morning,
       begged only for one
seed to be placed in the middle of a cold,
            faraway chapel. This is my way
            of crying don't you see that? A few men with hammers
      are putting on a new roof next door.
         Robert, your mama just called she
    sick. The drug dealers have moved into some
        other ether and I wanted very much
to say goodbye to the motherless one.
        I know that the sun has forgotten
        us but goddamn it,
    does it have to mock us too? The absence of sadness
        may create bitterness.

Further Problems with Pleasure

Friends, I'm going to leave Facebook to become a vegan and/or
astronaut. Flying high above my own sorcery, the police will never
helicopter-mom me! RJ spent the eighties
in Miami stealing cars but he was only the middle man so there's
something pathetic about that, no? Now he's in Alabama sitting in a tree swing
hunting deer so it makes me hate him. Once he got
arrested for stealing a sandwich from 7-11 and that's what did him in.
I want to know what he's thinking, then I don't.
Throw me in jail where I can write some poetry, I said.
He said throw me in jail so I stop stealing cars. The problem with pleasure
is that you need more and more of it to force it to
be more measurable and before you know it, it flips
to torture. A house, a palace
a mansion, a police car—imagine the possibilities. When someone
refers to "the poor," I turn into a trailer and Hurricane Rita
blows me away. Friends, I'm going to leave
Facebook to become a vegan.

Smoke Weed, Drink Coffee, Go Scalloping

Smoke weed, drink coffee, go scalloping.
   Conflicting desires: animation or just fall into the sofa?
The dominion of their blue eyes will cost
     them their dominion. Mixed media
of prehistoric flesh and saltwater. Benign substances drift.
     Friends in and out of the house. It was love but the slow kind; I had
to wait for you in jellyfish time. One week inside the Gulf of Mexico,
      the next in a borax mine. I reached into
the sea grasses for empty shells. *Loneliness*
      without rest! But to lift my hand even to boil
some water for tea. He shucked
the scallops. My body, either in txt or irl, ate silently.

Ode to Country Music

If I wasn't such a deadbeat, I'd learn Greek.
    I wouldn't write sonnets; I'd write epics
and odes. I'd love a man or woman who was
    acceptable, conformed to every code.
I'd finally put together my IKEA desk and write my epic or ode
    at sunset over my suburb. How I would love my shrubs!
But all I do is listen to country (and the occasional Joni)
    and smoke weed. Judge me judge me
judge me. Oh I've been through the shallows.
    I shallow. I hope. I hole. I know
I wrote you the most brutal love poem love knows.

Ode to Suicide, Delirium and Early REM

One time, I was on Twitter and Elisa or Anne or maybe it was on Facebook
posted this thing about the way the tips of your eyes point and I was disappointed
    because
mine are not almond-shaped, like my sister's, my tips are "downturned,"
        something medieval and sad, something fenced-in the manuscript or
           economic,
           the way they paint the little strawberries are a technological advance,
  and deep green vines up the gold-vermillion boxes to keep the text in, to keep
the lion in, to keep the flow
    of the blue flow robes in,
        Mine point down (Almond eye surgery for downturned eyes? please help,
        photos)
           the way Mary's tips point down, the hue, a libidinous blue,
a corruption, wave, metal star work of mournful
      space—opening onto the maze of resistance
        or the deep paralysis of a bad aesthetic, how to move on, how to
incorporate, my god, the bad frosted hair, the callous way you are supposed
to treat other humans to "get by," as in the cells swirling around
      a pool called "survival," I can't do anything else but
    this cranked-up harmony, this nerve a sort of beat, slot-machine
        or instinct the eyes point down and that is sad and there is no
          way
        around that but I could see right through you, I mean, I am you,
          or rats,
        or the way that horror itself is
  timed and gridded
   and paces around the manuscript too,
like a fabled beast not a real animal no something
      with horns from myth, from what has been passed down to scare
        the kids to keep them together

I walked & walked
    & walked & walked
                in the black and white forest, found a puff
                    of woodpecker feathers, made earrings from
                a body of flight and pounding
like an animal already deceased but he or she doesn't know it yet
    and neither do we, seeking shade the kind you throw on someone else
        this is the transport to
                torture, stateside, on a salty island, I said I'd write an ode
                        to suicide, delirium and early REM
                    in an ice chair, in the metallic clicks of brute force,
            inside our terrible century which isn't cryptic
at all, but encrypted in the omi-
    nous / anonymous
            transactions of bank
            errors, pirate's treasure behind glass in the Florida History
            Museum
and the little kids go "ohhhh" when they stick
    their puny heads, bouncing with coded ringlets, into one side
        of the model cannon, that's what Charlotte did (my little girl),
Helloooooo a man said at one end
        and Char said *Helloooooo*
    and my son and I were hanging on to the *ooooooo* like the creeping
vines on the manuscript

You are rich in grace but poor
    in destruction like cranes flying off for no reason, forming
    their tribute to nature and I thought
        to be beautiful, the eyes should point up
            because up signifies hope, goodness,
                the "white page" "white" "pure" "up," in control of the means
                    of production if not now
                      at some point
                in the future

For anything to be beautiful, really, it should strive
The way angels do
    The way gods do
The way cranes do
      The way human thought is supposed to do

Dear X,
  I have fucked up
Forgive me
  Or make me suffer in some way
these characters suffer
  in this manuscript
bound to their golden horns,
    to their encrusted two dimensions
to their tinted colors
    coagulating like blood
Like loss
  Like things I can't think of
That I can't be
  That I am
Like selves that splinter
  And every time I focus
on getting by I think
  Can't you leave me
to suffer
  Can't you go
inside your own
  tomb of longing,
your own Sappho-like box
  with a lid on top
Your own Sappho-like
  song box
with a strong song lid
  on top and a gold lock

Leave me to the glass heart this man
  placed in the palm of my hand
    on the bank of the Suwannee River
He said a preacher blessed it
and so I carry it around
in my jean jacket pocket and feel it
I want you to see it
    and feel it because it is smooth and ridiculous
because I can't bear to throw it away
      because it is over the top

of the box
and so Greek with lament
    that I want you to stay inside my lament
  and feel it
    because I am superstitious and I wish
my lament could be inside your
    head every day like the ocean
    that can't be depicted
      in the manuscript or the present moment
which Chris Kraus says radicalizes everything
  but I disagree I think it's the past
that radicalizes everything
    that is the strange light and the lid
and the box and the lock and the red glass

I am more ancient more atrocious
more volatile and laced with inconsistent abstractions
        stuffed with them like a lark or nature
      so I go downward
              like Ra is to rain
          interior of the sun
          "demons scatter
              in terror"

I'm going to make a big pot of chili this
weekend because I'm broke
       as fuck No matter what
       I go under the bank vault, under the cannon,
underneath the pigmented clouds, their blue veins bulging
           I have erased your box
             with this downwardness
I go under where it's just the intoxicating smell of money
     and rain and state buildings
and pulsating vines of ivy

I follow these downward tips
    my eye sockets
that are not beautiful after all
  but eternally plain
as coffins, organs,
    I want to survive
but I don't want to be inside them
   like a black bell
   like torture broken down
for what it is—
   a well or language spiral

Have Fun in France

With such
    unbearable melancholy, the poem sells,
      I mean sustains itself.
Nothing resurrects
      the poisonous present
          like this incantatory mood—lush,
            warned against, too many
          layers of gold leaf or a hermaphroditically
          florid description
               of space.

Ten weeks ago you posted
      a picture of your little boy
         holding a toy
      angel. The moon, background
      image and great destroyer, was a mere piece
      of tinsel wavering
         the galactic fit of
            an evening already lost, already
              hopelessly nostalgic. Oh
                you know this.
        The season
         flips over—
        an animal after
            an orgasm. Looks up. At what?
              The ceiling is
         exactly
         as it was.

Take all of your grammarians,
bunch them up like a bouquet of
laws, aestheticize their crass
existence
by endlessly referencing
them, those, it, they, whatever.

Nothing
flows from the law except
the last
river, abstracted from its own
source of fauna.

Abstracted
and denounced, the testimony
flung like seeds
into the flickering depth
of what some
call harmoniousness.

Further Problems with Pleasure

"Do not give up on your desire," but tell me something that will
destroy my life. The culture and the century are so entwined
so how are we going to break the hearts of the young?
I submit this here song to the trees! I submit to the summer
and all her lovers glistening like meat! I submit to the way sex propels
the engine forth! I submit to the organisms who shake their
fists and stomp their feet and the clouds with their
complex strategies! My lovers scatter before me,
how will I collect them? "Do not give up on your desire,"
but tell me the story of something that will.

Domestic Song

Cling to me
　　　　or don't
　　say anything
　　at all. Everyone consumed
　　　　　by the mirage complex.

　　We worked so hard on the formula
　　of the mattress. What color
　　　　　was it, though?
　　And did anyone count the flame tips

　　　　　when they rose over the patio, the garden?

　　　　I don't want to check the bank
　　　　　　account today. I'm afraid
　　　　　I've ruined us.

　　　　　The gnome's burnt
　　　　　　　torso against
　　　　　　the strawberries
　　　　　　in the clay pot.

Conceptual Poem

Conceptual Poetry is a life sentence of selfies shrugging
in a privatized prison The social role
of the poet was the most annoying girl in the class who cried and cried
all day and in the morning with a picket sign Something I don't know
a gang bang I don't want to say that honey He couldn't move past
his own pornography which was a problem that involved
trucks and generally being an idiot I think my ideas are good
here I'm afraid of art museums and IKEA Oh god I hate
IKEA and you and trucks and Tallahassee and who
is going to pay off all my student loans?

Psychedelic Garden Poem

I was thinking so much
about the *Songs of Innocence*, I swore
I woke up inside of them.
"I love my haters"; "Nature is..."
I relapsed on my pneumonia
because I drank wine and went running
in bad weather or did I swim
in Lake Paradise or ride a bicycle
into the forest or did I drive
past New Times Country Buffet?
At "Patients First," the walk-in clinic,
I got a prescription for a second round
of antibiotics called Augmentin.

In the waiting room,
I let a little girl watch a cartoon
bunny hop in a swamp on my phone.
Sound the flute! Now it's mute!
The nurse says I have a slight
fever, the mother says "thank you,"
Craig says you know they assume that
everyone who goes there is
a drug addict; the guy on TV
gives advice to a couple
on how to fix up their second home

and rent it out; the wife says she wants
short-term renters because
that way they can make more
money. The husband wants long-term renters—
it is a problem. Were my lungs
lying to me? Tofu and mashed potatoes,

my friend posts a picture on Facebook
and a stranger's status updates: "still kickin"
"so what you gonna do?" "in tha sticks"
"workin workin" "who wants to kick it?"
Why is it you can upload
a picture of your face and it only
looks pretty for a week or
two then it's on to the next
picture of your face slowly
dissolving and every poem seems

weaker than the next. I was convinced
this was the *Songs of Innocence*.
A philosopher tweeted about
taking his music records
through airport security: "I am
to my own heart merely
a serf" and inspected them closely
by wiping them with a cloth

became a medieval green
Sumer is icumen
inside the *Songs of Innocence*
and I was inside mold spores
on the wall of the apartment and side
effects include this garden
which is a kind of unpaid labor
as my voice right here singing to you
is also a kind of unpaid
labor and unpaved road
to the aquifer beneath my body
there is something that wants
to hold the world and it has nothing

to do with my pretty face
or my lungs which are failing
and full of rain and wine.

"The hart he loves
the high wood /the hare
she loves the hill" and "As I walked
by myself and talked
to myself." I can't remember
what happened but there were hawks
and my little boy was gone
and my daughter was old and everyone else
had dissipated into a thicket
the color which was a cross between
alpine rocks resolving
only to be harsh and cold air
over some scribbles of atmosphere.

Sometimes it is difficult
to think of the way something
should or shouldn't start.
A rare bacteria makes her entrance known
and then she is entirely the space
she displaces which is the weight
of the small lung
of a mouse. And as it loops back
on itself the hawk morphs into a second-
hand desire like wanting a character
to shoot himself because of his pure goodness
and nothing else. But this is
also how I knew that I was inside
the garden of No Bird Could Die Here
or mice or women or their miraculous songs.

The Elysian Fields

The people who drink themselves to death, cirrhosis or heart attack
    in a plastic lawn chair under the day moon and azaleas and those who blow
        their brains out or asphyxiate
    in a Prius—*is that possible?* Would the Prius give the desperate soul
a large enough carbon monoxide cloud to binge on death?
      Life is evil
      That is all
I want to live because I'm stubborn
        And even though my mind turns on my body, I'm a skinny little thing
    and nervous
      Help! These rich bankers are all committing suicide
        I even read an article about a CEO who shot himself with a nail
        gun
      Now that one understood the beauty of seeing
the Virgin Mary at the bottom of a swimming pool
          I cross my fingers every time I get on a train or plane
    I'm not like that though
Not the type to give in or up
    on other people or the eventual occasions
    for new disasters

At the junior college, Craig would go to one corner of
  the library where they kept the criminology books
    He read about a thirty-six-year-old man
found dead in his bed (nothing appeared unusual)
    He fell between the mattress
and the wall so intoxicated that he couldn't lift himself
    out of his stupid situation
A decade passes Craig tells me the same story
    and I say honey, I have already heard that story
    and he sort of shrugs or says, "Okay Okay so then, what's
    one more time?"

Why do you have to tell me the same
        gruesome stories over
and over but I like the fixation
        on the moment, to binge on the day moon
    and azaleas, febrile, galactic,
the afterglow of sex radiates through the house
The kids are watching Elmo and if I see another roach
        in the kitchen, I'm going to scream
        at the closest person to me oh that's my daughter, Charlotte
(Well, I can't scream at her!)

        My high school website has a page
of all the people who died so far
They rarely update it
        Some of the names seem vaguely familiar
Perhaps I passed one of them in the halls
    opening my locker getting out a book or lunch
I feel bad for their families
    I hope that they were bad people
dying so young adieu to the day moon
        I didn't believe you anyway
Being so full of delight and mystery

You were simply a hallucination
        like some spirit flung into a diamond waterfall at times
            motioning to the carbon fields how
did we trash it in the way that we did almost a Pompeii
        of the imagination Eliot's fisherman
            senile and meandering

    First the world on fire and then hardening
into place the hands the earthenware pots
        Poor babies—once someone told me that a baby
has the same size eyeball as an adult
    but this must be a lie

though an interesting lie
the baby sees bigness
and we grow
      myopic and weird

"People get weirder" a middle-
aged woman once told me when I was
      a teenager and also she said "he dressed
like he's straight from the eighties"

Think of the way forest moss creeps
      and crawls I hate
        architecture and the way the world
  has been built up around the flesh oh why can't
   the flesh be released to pure
      desire like blue blown silk
        over a rough ocean

The whites of the eyes like the white tops
      of waves you could collect
a bouquet of waves and give them
  to your sweetie for Valentine's Day
     but somehow architecture
     and its suggestion of cement and stasis
     is too powerful, too irresistible

There was one girl, Rachel, who died my senior year
     in a car crash on Lincoln Boulevard
       right next to the shop where they sold
      Piñatas and "Bow Wow! Wow!" the dog grooming place
She was alone in the car that day
    in 1993 and I remember in school the way
      her hair was blonde
     and feeble

like a tributary
　　　　to some secret
　　　　hideout
and Summer came up to me after fifth period
　　　　and said can you believe
what happened to Rachel Smith
　　　　and I said of course I can't believe it
and then Summer said well you know the family
　　is Mormon There are five other
brothers and sisters
　　　　so their parents will be okay

How did Summer know exactly what to say?
　　　　　even if it wasn't true
　　　I imagine the family wept every time they drove
　　　down Lincoln or saw
　　　　　　a piñata or dog
　　　Lincoln is such an ugly street
What it must mean
to lose your child on an ugly street versus
a very beautiful street

Which ancient philosopher thinks that life is
　　　　　　a rehearsal for death?
　　　　Or is that something from bullshit New Age
mysticism I read at
　　the hippie crystal shop I love? The suicides reverse it—
They think that death is a rehearsal
for flowers—specifically
　　　　　the night blooming ones
with their unusual shapes that stretch and elongate time
or curb language with
　　　　　their faint aromas

I would like to plant at least ten night blooming flowers
         in the next few weeks
because they are mysterious and not particularly happy
         I think it is unwise
to be a "happy poet"
         Just as it is unwise to be a "nice poet"
Or what about the vague insult of being a
         "hard-working poet"

My stalker says that I am is fat and need plastic
         surgery I have to check her Twitter
         feed regularly to see how
              I'm doing
              "This is Illyria, lady."
"And what should I do in Illyria?"
                   "My brother he is in Elysium"
              Or the asylum? Or the walled-garden?

Why not sit and stay a while
in the rolling waters of
  these alcohol-dipped words
              and talk about the glass bottles
         of childhood? Things pass,
              even disturbed things pass
         the edges mellow
                   the memory mellows too
  and that is
         a good thing

Or let's disturb these woodpeckers
with our talk of this and that
or throw
         rocks into the pool?

"Elysium Mons" is the name
    given to a volcanic region
of Mars My son asks
    if I will accompany him to Mars
on a spaceship
    No, Ezekiel
Mars isn't for me
And anyway, I will be too old
(and I'm a horrible claustrophobe!)
I like it right here
under this dome
    talking to you, honey,
For better or for worse
This is my colored garden

A Poem for Alex

This flight is very short—thirty-seven minutes
to be exact. My friend said that when you get
to where you think the poem is going
to end, try to keep pushing it
a bit further.

Okay, but why?

To get to the blue meat of things.
The clouds are blue and meaty today, silver
at the edges and lined with fat.

I wish I was a traveling salesman.
I would sell frozen steaks and I would knock
at someone's door and then pull the hard
steaks out of the blue cooler
and scream, "Somebody wants you!"
and then the person wouldn't know
what to do so, naturally,
she would buy all the steaks
and then I would wheel the empty cooler home
like I had done something important that day.

I just looked at a picture of you
on my phone and it made me smile because
your name is so long and Greek
and I will probably never be able
to spell it. For someone as intelligent
as I am, I'm a really bad speller. Are you?

I sometimes like it when things are short
and sweet like this flight and I also
like it sometimes when things are long, difficult,
full of nauseating waves
like that ferry ride we took from Athens to Crete.
The thing is is that a poem, when written just
right can seduce or transport a lover
or often both. You don't have to be mysterious
or buoyant like we were so young but
now accustomed to manipulating language
the world becomes sweet, malleable and oh look—
there's the Minoan snake goddess now
with her ancient, explosive powers.

Alex, are we old now? I know there
are stories beneath these bodies of ours, lots of sorrow
like spirals of sparrows you see painted
on the walls of the old world made of tears,
regret, longing, accomplishment
but these bodies, they are still ours, right, at least
for a bit longer, though different?

I guess I'm being sentimental,
which is unusual. The dazzling earth below scares
the shit out of me and the dazzling stars above do too.
But I believe you, like metaphor
that, in the end, collapses into itself, revealing
the only dimension it ever was—one thing—
some raw truth like clouds or steak.

Further Problems with Pleasure

I like the way you look a little depressed. Anyone here got anything
for me to suck on? Shouldn't down bottles of red wine:
I'm a drum on the run I'm a bummer a sad sack of brain matter.
Do all your boys know about each other? I've got some venison
in the freezer. Sometimes I read your poems at work and it makes
me feel better but when you say the word "cunt," I have to
close my browser. I've neglected my
studies. I've neglected to wash the baby socks.
I like the way you look depressed staring out from your
Facebook prison maybe we can talk? Am I creepy? Am I horny?
Anyone here got anything for me to suck on?

Two Sarahs

Nor have I ever watched the contrails of jets
      from a palm tree and coral reef resort,
        sequestered on a Caribbean island shaped
      like a common button mushroom
like Sarah. "It's never scary for me," she says.

  When the seagulls congregate
around the thin wrapper of a Snickers bar, the mother
    squawking at her babies, I imagine there must be something gullible
      in the very forms of nature, the way capital flows
        in the sky—streamlined,
    consistent, if even for the occasional
      turbulent interlude. Everything versus how
     we behaved on the ground
(looters, robbers, rapists), which is mostly tragic.

  I find the entire plot of land
  guarded by land and wire excessively sorrowful. Or am
I mistaken? Is the sky sorrowful too and the land
    a funerary urn? Ornate, childish, like spoiled little rich girls
          who hate each other yet deserve each other
so one wonders why they can't kiss
    and make up, jump into
      a cab and go to the party where they'll meet
        more of themselves and drink
          the world into drained bank accounts.

And at the moment when the poem
      becomes most poignant, when the terrifying
   premonition has fulfilled
   the contours of the wish, when all that mattered

converged on that one hint, when the poet suddenly realizes
     she has slowly
and successfully backed away from the cruelty
    of the sun, she sweetly brings
       the title back into her poem and says in a whisper
      "Two Sarahs," so everyone
        knows she has won.

August in South Georgia

Why do I drink so much gin? Has something to do
with the way they burn the trees down here on either
side of the highway. Man selling boiled peanuts,
man selling handmade canoes. If you know the south,
you know a good woman can only really get the blues
in the winter. Summer is meant for losing weight. No white
people are going to talk about race. The Goodwood Plantation
I drive by every day has no memory—all those baby
alligators and volunteer tour guides with their quaint anecdotes
that lodge in your throat like the demented sun.

In This Version

there's an impulse for privacy though I realize
that testimony streams from every delightful
                    opening the body
                                has to offer.

            Or if the narrator is guilty, so be it.
        I can tell from your profile
you like hiking, parrots,
                    and you're afraid of getting old.

        I am too. Who isn't?
                Only the young
                            who will never
                know what pleasure could
                have been.

    As if pleasure isn't
        historical. As if our bodies
        are not tightened, thinned,
    or relaxed according to
dictators, bureaucrats,
                    the inventors
                    of trans fat.

        They don't know
        what we go through, and defending
                    pleasure kills it
                    before the judge
                        can render
                            a verdict.

Farewell, Mississippi, farewell.
         If it was a game,
    you won, if it wasn't,
              I'm embarrassed to say
    you turned me on.

The needless battles,
              the false posture
              of glory, defeat,
              the pathetic spectacle.

              There was no terrorist
              among us but you
    imagined the worst
    in everything and took us
         all down with you.

The Women

I don't know what women want, Eileen.
    Maybe love. Maybe the tops of alpine
trees, light blue and shivering
        under a mad snowfall.

The woman sitting next to me
        on this plane is reading a hardback
romance novel. On the cover,

a girl with flowing black hair
    is dressed in a long red cape
and the red cape is flowing too
    in the blue, blue wind.

I get scared to fly through air.
    I guess I fear a lot of things.

When women hate me, I recoil
    like ugliness itself and all I've ever
wanted is some motherly presence
        to make tea for me with steam flowing
out of the top of the ceramic mug to say
        everything will be okay.

I lean over and look at her book.
    The first line in chapter one
says the book takes place
    in California in 1850.

She notices the intrusion, says, "It's a book
        about self-love. The main character grew up
in a rough environment and was
        treated like a sex slave
and then became a prostitute."

I pour a glass of red wine
        and this violent atmosphere is going
to break my heart open today
        like a piece of luggage—out spills

the history of my life like lots
of dresses, books, lotions,
        leggings, electric blue makeup.

I relate to Celan's poetry,
        that terrible, sad search for a mom—
        screwed up and convoluted like
a knot in the throat of bruised trees.

Dear Chris

Life is hard. We don't need art to say so.
            Life is hard. Do you know
                that great Dickinson line
            where she says she walked
from "plank to plank"? Or maybe she leapt,
        like a flame, the light at one
                with the wavering scene,
cryptic and serene as known emotion.
    Sometimes, on one of my late night
        experimental walks, I get the urge to smoke
            cigarettes and look for owls in our dying trees
                and oh yeah,
                    revolution. Oh yeah.

And the source of my sadness is . . .
And the great ravines of my sadness are . . .

But we have to hash it out in this world,
    which is bullshit, like Fiona said,
            in her MTV speech in the nineties, and then
she got called the "crazy girl"
        "the anorexic girl" but I think
            some of us really are witches, the ones who feed
            their kids Chicken McNuggets
after work because we are so tired
    and we actually want
to be poets and we know we can't break
    through this world by ourselves, no,
        none of us can push our flesh through the wreckage
we made, I mean we didn't fucking make this, the makers did,
            we were just living poem

to poem, paycheck to pay-
            check, god I'm always in
debt, little kiss on the cheek goodbye for the day
my darling, loving each other, like gifted but confused
        animals, paint this day,
                a painting of emotional
weaponry, I am an army too, feverish, past
reason, it is Shakespeare's
        birthday today, it is my son's birthday
today I make this poem
            instead of cupcakes
for his class, my little angel, forgive me, don't be
mad, this poem is not a cupcake.

It contains no sugar. It is not a loving aria
        either, it is the bitters
            of the victors, us, the future composite
            of us, looking back
            on our future, I won't be here, Chris
        you won't Anne won't Joshua won't
You won't be there Ezekiel won't be there
                but it will be there
        It will start like this, the beginning of *La Traviata*,
    but she won't die so many deaths, Rufus won't
                have to sing about us dying
            our womanly deaths, she won't need to resurrect either,
an irritation that grows into its fire, and take the form
            of any desire that we need....Civilization is coming!
            Okay, I'm kidding about that.

Even in the whipping sounds
    of subjectivity, the windy terrain of it,
            inside those whipping sounds
        of the cold, silvery atmosphere, sci-fi

and metallic, even then,
                we are bound to our conflicts, promises,
            resolutions, revolutionary
impulses, and the more ancient
            understandings too, like fate.

But also *fuck reality*, as Anne says in her long wig
            and cancer. *Fuck reality*. This
        is ours. Fuck it. Fuck reality. This too is ours.
                Under the strobe light. Under the gay moon,
            the queer moon. We deserve this; it is ours too.
    These are our bodies.
                They are ours.
            We can do
            what we want, the poet said, but in that optimism,
            the tidal wave of repression,
    consolidation, despair, my own despair
which is the pep talk I give myself
            every morning to keep going,
            but we pushed back on it, the despair,
    we were few and we pushed hard and we did this
        even though we were, among us,
            not equals. Not me and you, Chris.
    We are not equals. But we pushed back on it
        regardless, together. We did. Let it
                be known. We did this. Very little
                happened. We did this.

A canopic jar in the form
        of a demi-god. *I look in my casket*
        and miss a pearl. The silent
way of love like a picture of pure wheat
    against the aquarium sky. It's comic, the way
            our emoji linger
                in my sphere of longing. This is the way

the wilderness is formed, I can't begin to tell you
        but everything threatens it, technology, a dick pic,
to take magic and crunch the numbers,
        load it with precarity, so hang out
        on a lawn and read
the poems of a recently dead
        comrade, see the comrade in death, against that
clear-eyed anthology of power.

In the cult of the sun worshippers, we were messy
        in the mansions of Ka, death is before me
        today, under your Yew tree, Plath-like and real,
but it is also a joyous thing, to look out on it like this,
"Death is before me today, Chris Nealon"
        on my son's birthday,
        but it isn't dangerous.

Wait a second. She stepped. Now I
        remember. She didn't walk. She didn't
leap. She didn't
        run. She stepped. And you know
how she did it? Slow and
        cautiously. So, basically, she didn't know
        what was going to happen. She didn't know
how it would all go down. But then, that's what
experience actually is. Knowing,
        not knowing, proceeding, the pep talk.

I hope my son and daughter are your son's comrades.
Why hope?
They will be.
We will make it so.
I should say this again to you.
We will make it so.

Acknowledgments

American Poetry Review: August in South Georgia, Dear Chris, The Elysian Fields, Ode to Delirium, Our Lady of Perpetual Help, Poetry Is Stupid and I Want to Die

The Awl: A Poem for Criminals and Construction Workers, The Woman with the Foreign Accent

Chicago Review: Psychedelic Garden Poem, A Song for Paperweights, Have Fun in France

Poets.org (Academy of American Poets Website): Ode to Country Music, A Poem for Joe

Boston Review: In This Version, Two Sarahs

Lana Turner: A Journal of Poetry and Opinion: Allegory, Damned Ladies, Destruction, Fun Clothes: A Gothic, Spring Dirge

The Brooklyn Rail: Further Problems with Pleasure 1-6, A Lover's Discourse

Hyperallergic: Smoke Weed, Drink Coffee, Go Scalloping

Spoon River Review: A Poem for Alex, The Women

Interim: Eternity, Exotic Perfume, Metamorphosis of the Vampire, My Sexuality Is "Victim of Capitalism," The Sick Muse

The Iowa Review: The Albatross, Jewels, The Possessed

Sandra Simonds is the author of several collections of poetry including *Steal It Back* (Saturnalia Books, 2015), *The Sonnets* (Bloof Books, 2014), *Mother Was a Tragic Girl* (Cleveland State University Poetry Center, 2012) and *Warsaw Bikini* (Bloof Books, 2009). Her poems have been anthologized in *The Best American Poetry* 2014 and 2015. She is a professor of English and Humanities at Thomas University in Thomasville, Georgia.